So Far So Good

Also by Ursula K. Le Guin

Ursula K. Le Guin

So Far So Good

FINAL POEMS: 2014–2018

Copper Canyon Press

Port Townsend, Washington

Cover art: Lisa Gilley, *Yakima Canyon* (Yakima River, WA), 2013, oil on wood, 60" × 60". http://www.lisagilley.com.

Copper Canyon Press is in residence at Fort Worden State Park in Port Townsend, Washington, under the auspices of Centrum. Centrum is a gathering place for artists and creative thinkers from around the world, students of all ages and backgrounds, and audiences seeking extraordinary cultural enrichment.

LIBRARY OF CONGRESS CATALOGING-IN-PUBLICATION DATA
Names: Le Guin, Ursula K., 1929–2018, author.
Title: So far so good : Final Poems: 2014–2018 / Ursula K. Le Guin.
Description: Port Townsend, Washington : Copper Canyon Press, [2018]
Identifiers: LCCN 2018016185 | ISBN 9781556595387 (hardback : alk. paper)
Classification: LCC PS3562.E42 A6 2018 | DDC 811/.54—dc23
LC record available at https://lccn.loc.gov/2018016185

9 8 7 6 5 4 3 2 FIRST PRINTING

COPPER CANYON PRESS
Post Office Box 271
Port Townsend, Washington 98368

www.coppercanyonpress.org

ACKNOWLEDGMENTS

Ursula sent off her revised manuscript for *So Far So Good* for copyediting on January 15, 2018. She died January 22. This book, then, is the last collection of her poetry she would edit; it is her farewell.

In creating these poems, Ursula worked in the illimitable space of her own imagination, yet always grounded and surrounded by her family and friends: by Charles most of all; by her children and grandchildren—Elisabeth, Lyra, Theo, Nancy, India, Isabel, Chip, Caroline, Rick; by Vonda, Katherine, Katie, Moe and George (and his oatcakes); by the Poetry group—Barbara, Bette, Jeannette, Kari, Molly, Noel—through which many of these poems passed in the process of coming to completion. And, of course, by Pard.

Bringing this book through to its final form has been the work of many hearts and hands, including Ginger Clark and Michael Wiegers and John Pierce at Copper Canyon Press.

And it seems fitting to acknowledge Ursula's gratitude for the gift of words, a gift she never took for granted over a long lifetime—these words of hers, never wholly hers, that now she gives to you.

Caroline Le Guin
March 2018

CONTENTS

Observations

Incantations

Meditations

Elegies

The Night Journey

So Far

In the Ninth Decade

So Far So Good

Observations

Little Grandmother

A dry-voiced chickadee
reproves what's gone amiss.
From our crab-apple tree
she gazes critically
at autumn's entropy
and quietly says this:
I am Chickadee,
and things have gone amiss.

Words for the Dead

Mouse my cat killed
grey scrap in a dustpan
carried to the trash

To your soul I say:

With none to hide from
run now, dance
within the walls
of the great house

And to your body:

Inside the body
of the great earth
in unbounded being
be still

McCoy Creek: Cattle

Long after sunset the afterlight
glows warm along the rimrock.
A wind down off the mountain
blows soft, a little chill.
I've come to love the quiet sound
cattle make cropping short grass.
Day and night are much the same
to them in the pastures of summer,
cows and calves, they crop and pull
with that steady, comfortable sound
as the light in the rimrock and the sky
dims away slowly. Now no wind.
I don't know if cattle see the stars,
but all night long they graze
and walk and stand in the calm
light that has no shadows.

Merlin

I

Her feathery raiment and the July sun
made her a glory as she flew,
a blaze of gold and white
dappled with dun against the blue.
Instant as a meteor she claimed the sky,
jinked, veered, towered to soar
above the hill, and disappeared,
crying her piercing, hissing cry.

II

Mice in the dry roots of the grasses
     on the sunlit hill
crouched when that shadow passed.
Small birds down by the creek
     were still,
 hearing the dragon speak.

All Saints All Souls

This is the day when the saints all go
silently to church in France
and over the mountains of Mexico
the bare bones dance.
Ghosts rise up from graveyard sleep
to follow the southward-fleeing sun.
It is the doomsday of the leaf,
the feast day of the skeleton.

McCoy Creek: Wind

The wind beats on the drums
of my ears and overturns the chairs,
blowing out of all the years
we've come here, been here.

The bird that says *tzeep* says *tzeep*.
Dry pods on the old honey locust rattle.
Barbed wire draws straggling lines between
us and distant cattle.
Rocking like little white sailboats
two hens cross the footbridge.

Behind me and before me
the basalt ridges are silent
as the air is silent when
the wind for a moment ceases.

Six Quatrains

AUTUMN

gold of amber
red of ember
brown of umber
all September

MCCOY CREEK

Over the bright shallows
now no flights of swallows.
Leaves of the sheltering willow
dangle thin and yellow.

OCTOBER

At four in the morning the west wind
moved in the leaves of the beech tree
with a long rush and patter of water,
first wave of the dark tide coming in.

SOLSTICE

On the longest night of all the year
in the forests up the hill,
the little owl spoke soft and clear
to bid the night be longer still.

THE WINDS OF MAY

are soft and restless
in their leafy garments
that rustle and sway
making every moment movement.

HAIL

The dogwood cowered under the thunder
and the lilacs burned like light itself
against the storm-black sky until the hail
whitened the grass with petals.

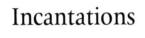

Incantations

Come to Dust

Spirit, rehearse the journeys of the body
that are to come, the motions
of the matter that held you.

Rise up in the smoke of palo santo.
Fall to the earth in the falling rain.
Sink in, sink down to the farthest roots.
Mount slowly in the rising sap
to the branches, the crown, the leaf-tips.
Come down to earth as leaves in autumn
to lie in the patient rot of winter.
Rise again in spring's green fountains.
Drift in sunlight with the sacred pollen
to fall in blessing.
                           All earth's dust
has been life, held soul, is holy.

On Second Hill

Where on this wild hill alone
a child watched the evening star,
let these bits of ash and bone
rejoin the earth they always were,
the earth that let her sing her love,
the gift that made the giver
here on the lonely hill above
the valley of the river.

Lullaby

where's my little fleeting cat
a year a year an hour a day
where's my little girl at
fleeting away sleeping away
found the way clear away
nowhere far nowhere near
a day a day an hour a year

To the Rain

Mother rain, manifold, measureless,
falling on fallow, on field and forest,
on house-roof, low hovel, high tower,
downwelling waters all-washing, wider
than cities, softer than sisterhood, vaster
than countrysides, calming, recalling:
return to us, teaching our troubled
souls in your ceaseless descent
to fall, to be fellow, to feel to the root,
to sink in, to heal, to sweeten the sea.

Travelers

I

We came from the far side of the river
of starlight and will cross back over
in a little boat
no bigger than two cupped hands.

II

Thinking about compassion.
A firefly in a great dark garden.
An earthworm naked
on a concrete path.

III

I think of the journey
we will take together
in the oarless boat
across the shoreless river.

Meditations

There was a jar in Oregon

not this time in Tennessee,
on which I set a crimson pear
without a reason but to see
the charm of chance propinquity.

The Fine Arts

Judging beauty, which is keenest,
Eye or heart or mind or penis?
Lust is blindest, feeling kindest,
Sight is strongest, thought goes wrongest.

An Autumn Reading

for Andrea

The poet read in the Scholar's Room
in the Chinese garden, her words
half heard in rush and crash of rain
on formal ponds and pavements,
like verses cut in an old stone
blurred by moss and lichen.
Under the downpour purple
chrysanthemums nodded in silence.

"There is always something watching you"

Eight bright bits of jet in the head
of a tiny spider hidden in cracked veneer.
Eye of a goldfish from its clear element
to which ours is all depths and vanishings.
The triple mirror in the half-lit hall
dwindling by repetition into its own dark.
A telescope across the city or on Aldebaran.
Your jealous god. Your neighbor's sad desire.
The sun itself, whose eye you only meet
briefly, as it begins to turn away.
The old ghost in your room
you've never seen, although it visits
timidly, sometimes.
The forest where you've lost your way,
though it knows where you are going.

Outsight

I'm half unseen,
to me, my skin
a screen
to all within.
My eyes can see a star,
but not my mind.
The more I think, the more
I am unfamiliar.
Insight is half blind
and surface-bounded.
Where is my core?
What inwardnesses are
unseen, unsounded?

Lesser Senses

Thinking of beauty
as sight we keep forgetting
    the warmth of the fire
in the brightness of firelight,
in graceful ripples the grace

of water to thirst.
Soft as air, the touch of fur
    on the touching hand
is as beautiful surely
as the curve of the cat's leap.

No keener beauty
than a dry branch of sagebrush,
    the harsh, poignant scent
bringing the silent desert
distances back to the heart.

A Cento of Scientists

Alternating lines from Charles Darwin,
Galileo Galilei, and Giordano Bruno

There is grandeur
The sun with all the circling planets it sustains
God is glorified and the greatness of his kingdom made manifest
in this view of life
the sun with all the circling planets yet
glorified not in one but in countless suns
from so simple a beginning endless forms
the sun with all the planets it sustains yet can ripen a bunch
    of grapes
not in a single earth, a single world, but in a thousand thousand
endless forms most beautiful and most wonderful
the sun can ripen a bunch of grapes as if it had nothing else in
    the universe to do
not in a single world but in a thousand thousand, an infinity
    of worlds
endless forms most beautiful and most wonderful have been
    and are being evolved
as if it had nothing else in the universe to do
All things are in the universe, and the universe is in all things,
    we in it and it in us
There is grandeur in this view of life

How it Seems to Me

In the vast abyss before time, self
is not, and soul commingles
with mist, and rock, and light. In time,
soul brings the misty self to be.
Then slow time hardens self to stone
while ever lightening the soul,
till soul can loose its hold of self
and both are free and can return
to vastness and dissolve in light,
the long light after time.

Elegies

It Used to Be

It used to be the shine of streetlights
on a rain-wet street was winter
and summer was outdoors and most of the time.
A season's slant of light noticed only
in August on the golden knolls, the hint
of ending, *to love that well*. . . The moon
was full and half and full and gone again
just as it pleased. Mostly the wind blew sweet
in off the Bay, but not the rare,
dry, bare north wind, the earthquake wind.
Sea fog, dear fog, came drifting in the Golden Gate
sometime in the afternoon and in the year
and was everywhere a while, the garden dripped
in a grey hush, then it was all gone.

I am wise to the seasons now. I foretell an altered light,
observe the Solstice and the Equinox,
am eased by the majestic order. I am old.
Yet still when fog from the river rises
silent and unforeseen, and the bright morning is all gone
into the uncreated, I rejoice.

Berkeley, December 1941

Imagine! blackout curtains in that house
with all its tall bright windows south and west!
They were of some opaque-brown stuff that fit
close to the frame. We must have drawn them down
each evening, raised them up again each day.
I don't remember doing that. I do recall
the first night, being scared and unprepared.
Only my parents' bedroom had any curtains,
and hardly thick enough to hide a light
from enemies in air above the sea,
so in the dark house, the dark city, we
all seven sat there round the Franklin stove
in the warm cave a single candle built
from shadows with its flame. And Alfred read
the bible to us. We were as irreligious
as coyotes, and I don't know what he read,
but it was great, and grave, and suitable
to that strange night, the first night of a war.
　　　And I remember when we took the blackout
curtains down, years later, how we stood
a long time looking at the patterned lights
of our bright cities, and the first calm stars.

Theodora

I think how fine my mother was.
Her doings and her things were lovable.
Her turquoise bracelets, her violet
dinner dress with a jeweled waist.
The way when she was undressing
she'd go around with her nylons unhitched.
I think of all this now with tenderness
and comfort in the recollection.

Oh I was so angry at her when she died
for dying, but at last that's gone
and she comes to me again with silver
and turquoise on her wrists
in the sunlight.

Felled

Sterile gravel, stepping stones
where the great willow grew.
Only to me in empty air
a tree I must walk through.

Rift

Looking at you over on that other side
of the rift that you decreed
between us, I'm scared to see
how hard, how fast the run of years
scours such a channel. Miles
across now. I can't tell how deep.

Talking, laughing, in the shade of the cedars

Bright and broad at the wide bend,
that was a kinder river, where grace was.
Still the shadowy-sunny water
from a spring the color of peacocks
is flowing on down through the forest
a long way from this desert canyon.

Talking, laughing, in the shade of the cedars

For Heggaia

When you lived in the Valley of the Na
and were a goldsmith
you made a little disc of gold, the sun
on one side, the double spiral
on the other, for Intrumo of Sinshan.
After you left, she wore it
on a golden chain, the rayed sun shining outward
the hinge of the spiral hidden against her throat.
Pretty soon she'll follow you
through that open doorway,
and coming by your workshop
near the bank of the River Na
smile to see you working.
"So you are here," you'll say,
and she, "Go along easily,
Heggaia of my heart!
I left your sun there in the other Valley
for us to find some day."

Bats

When I used to see bats flying
in the California twilight
their intricate zigzag voices
went flickering with them
but they fell silent with the years
and without that tiny sonar static
to see them flicker
in and out of being
is a kind of blindness

II

In the twilight in my dream
a little bat was flying
and awakening I wondered
if the bat that I remembered
flying in the twilight
of the dream of California
was in California or the dream.

After the Death of Orpheus

The rocks his song had moved, the wild
creatures that had gathered to him,
grieved as the echo of his song
followed the river into silence.

His shade stood awhile bewildered
at the shadowy door. At last
he went in and saw the downward way.
He had gone that way before
yet it could not be familiar.
Did he know the slight figure waiting
beside the pathway for him?

She turned and went ahead,
unspeaking. He followed her.
She did not turn around.
She led him down the vast descent
of twilight to the shore
where the old boatman waited,
received his payment,
and rowed them slowly over.

There was nothing to be said.

Under the weightless boat
the waters of shadow ran silent
towards the beginning of all music.

July

Sun warms the lizard's back
and the humble back of the mountain.
A raven croaks from the top of a thermal.
The valley oak above the barn,
dying a huge branch at a time,
stands in calm mortality, content
with the warm light that has fed its leaves,
the dark waters that have fed its roots,
its acorns that have fed the woodpeckers
for five hundred rainy seasons.

Looking Back

Remember me before I was a heap of salt,
the laughing child who seldom did
as she was told or came when she was called,
the merry girl who became Lot's bride,
the happy woman who loved her wicked city.
Do not remember me with pity.
I saw you plodding on ahead
into the desert of your pitiless faith.
Those springs are dry, that earth is dead.
I looked back, not forward, into death.
Forgiving rains dissolve me, and I come
still disobedient, still happy, home.

The Night Journey

Wakeful

Islanded

Snow and silence in the streets.
Winter in the bone.
In silent houses people sleep
each one alone.
Self-islanded by thought and dream
the solitary soul
forgets the deepest depth, the earth
that joins us all.

Night Voices

I

The great metal cattle of the train yards
bawl and bawl across the city in the darkness
cows calling their lost calves
from farther and farther

II

All night the black rain
on the cold pane
whispers, whispers,
we are your sisters

Noctis oceanus

The small, dark hours pass by, unlighted ships
far out on a starlit sea,
shadows through dim radiance. No origin,
no destination. Slip by and are gone.

If my mind could go on with them
into the compassless unending night,
boat with no harbor, hunter with no prey.

What I sought in voyaging I found,
the gifts I asked were given. Now

discoveries turn mystery, gift is loss.

Out beyond the gains and ends,
is only the voyage in starlight.

If I could know this fearlessly,
give up and give away, be easy and rejoice
that the little I knew was everything.

But darkness ebbs, its unity
yields to the dividing sun, unrisen yet already
sketching the architectures of the light
faint and inexorable on the shores of day.

Falling

Company

A paw, a questing nose half waken me,
and I let him get under the covers.
He curls up and purrs himself asleep.
Cats are less troublesome than lovers.

Doze

The little stone my mind
slips into the cloudy pond
and slowly settles in the silt
at the bottom of the water it could be forever

Farther

Adrift adrift
on the sound of rain
on a windless sea
in a sailless skiff

Sleep

The way it comes unnoticed, so easily.
Like when we were on the tide flats
of the great bay, a long time ago now,
the two girls wandering out between me
and the far-off, glittering water,
each of us crouching at a rock pool
absorbed, and then another rock pool,
till I looked up and saw the shine of water
between black rocks and weed wrack
where there had been only sand,
saw how it covered up the rocks
so easily, a rising as soft as sinking.
And the little one too far away to hear.
Her sister and I ran towards her,
calling, hollering, finally she looked up,
stood up, and struggled back to us
through quick-flowing, deepening water.
We splashed through shallows to the sand,
stood, turned, watched the glittering tide
rocking where we had been out there,
the other element:
                    where, to be, we must be other.
There all we know we must know differently,
in vastnesses, abysses, in shifting images,
in silences, illusions, monsters, gleams,
and always, under all, the dark,
and the peaceful sinking deeper as it rises.

Dreaming

Tracks

Strange are the ways and tracks of dreams
mind follows in its nightly wanderings.
The Syrian girls, their dark and timid eyes.
We gave the eggs to them. I finally found
the furry nest the cat had made
in the bank of dirt below the tennis court.
How glad I was to see him there and safe
from the strangers who'd taken over the house
and the coyotes everywhere. The eggs were all
painted with red dots and curlicues.
Connections vanish as I wake, but still
the little pawprints on the hidden track
into the nest are comforting to me.

The People

Some people have begun to come into my dreams
from a long way away,
traveling over the mountain passes
that nobody living knows.
Old people who smell like fog
and the soft bark of redwoods.
They talk together softly.
They know more than I know.
I think they come from home.

Waking

Seaward

foam on the low waves
morning dreams go drifting out
with the tide of light
vanishing as bubbles do
beings of air and water

seafoam my memory
is also   evanescent
spindrift from wave crests
white manes of the white horses
blown by the land-wind seaward

dreams memories all
becoming immaterial
the self unselving
gone adrift on the same tide

So Far

So Far

The metaphor (not the subject) of these
twelve poems is Lt. William Bligh's
navigation of an overloaded open boat
four thousand miles from Tonga past the
Australian coast to Timor in Maritime
Southeast Asia.

1. Planning

I set out on the everyday
with a watchful heart,
sunset
my only harbor.

I've lost my ship,
the command I led
and all her cargo.
I have this instead.

We've enough water
if we take care
and enough bread
to share.

Reefs to larboard
forbid the coast.
I steer the wind's way
always west.

What is ahead
is wave after wave
night after day
far, and farther.

I hope to chart
this unknown shore
and the long way yet
to Timor.

11. The Boat

Well built but heavy laden
with the weight of our mortality
she clambers struggling up a swell,
a moment hangs aloft
in sight of all the bright horizon,
slips down to the unstable valley
to labor up and up again.
Five inches of freeboard,
the breadth of my hand.

III. The Food

Rage was my privilege.
I didn't count its cost.
I've lost my anger
with the rest I lost.

Now my privilege
as I weigh out rations
of shred and crust
is a hungry patience.

Anger lays waste,
hunger saves and is fed.
I wait, and crave,
and am blest to have
my crust, my shred.

iv. The Unknown Continent

We are passing the great dry land
far south within the reefs.
Of its people we know only
we don't understand each other
and ignorance is danger.
We dare not come ashore
save on the outmost islands
briefly, to seek water.
I am used to being lonely
but forever to be a stranger
is a strange grief.

v. The Absolution

Times between responsibilities
when I am not at the tiller
or bailing, but can be still a while,
the vastness slowly enters deep
intaken with my breath.
A quiet attention to all things.
Unselved. Absolved.
I wish it could continue so.
But we are overloaded
and always in danger
and I so need to sleep when I can sleep.

VI. Calm Sea

The boat is poised
on a column of water
miles high
from seafloor to daylight.
She rests, supported.

If she were whelmed
the great column
would still bear her,
lowering her slowly
to rest in silence.

VII. The Course Kept

We go as we go
because the wind blows so
in this region of the seas
in this season of the year.
We lack the means
to turn our sail, to back and fill,

to catch or spill the breeze
choosing the way we will,
taking the tack we please,
as once we did, or thought we did.
We go as we are sent
and do as we are bid,
obedient.

VIII. Timor

The little Latin that I know
tells me timor means fear.
Timor is where I go.
There's no more land, no rest
between me and the west.
And day and night I steer
straight there, for what I fear
is not that landfall:

to lose my way
as I lost my command,
lose strength of hand
so I cannot steer,
the compass of the mind
till no way is left
and blindly day
and night nowhere
to no end drift.

IX. Intimations

My bare foot-soles
on the bare planking
are aware
of abyss and chasm.

Sometimes I feel
a tremor, a groping
upward beneath me

as if great beings
of the great deeps
were mutely seeking
me as I seek them.

x. The Boat Itself

The boat itself
the boat myself
alone
my crew my life
that I have never known

XI. Night

Between the blazing firmament
and the black abyss we are
in the mercy of the wind
that moves us on
through darkness over images of stars
between elements not ours.

Earth made our body,
rock made our bone.
Ocean is no man's country.
Heaven is not my home.
O may we come at last to land
in the mercy of the wind.

XII. Westering

From sunrise the wind blows
always to sunset
going where the stars go

my breath the wind

this little boat my body
its ragged sail my soul

going where the stars go

In the Ninth Decade

Three Quatrains

OVER EIGHTY

The wire
gets higher
and they forget
the net

MATTER

In dream I'm quick on my feet as I used to be,
running up and down stairs with a light clatter,
walking free not even knowing that I'm free,
not yet mastered by my own dark matter.

THE HARE

The hare that dwells on the hill of delight
even in wintry age will not turn white.
Thinner, but as lively as before,
she springs and dances at Aphrodite's door.

Theory of Aging

As the number of the year gets bigger
the year itself grows smaller
but heavier. It acquires gravity.
It will finally get so heavy
that it cannot continue as it is
but implodes to a black hole
into which sink all the years
becoming numberless
and utterly weightless.

The Old Novelist's Lament

I miss the many that I was,
my lovers, my adventurers,
the women I went with to the Pole.
What was mine and what was theirs?
We were all rich. Now that I share
the cowardice of poverty,
I miss that courage of companionship.
I wish they might come back to me
and free me from this cell of self,
this stale sink of age and ills,
and take me on the ways they knew,
under the sky, across the hills.

All Abroad

No need of Como now, or unseen
long-dreamed-of Sicily,
or to behold once more
except in dream the Hebrides,
when every morning opens on a shore
more foreign than any morning used to seem.
The world may be as it used to be
but I am altered, I the eye that sees
all half known, half strange as if newborn
and fresh to its mortality.

Leaves

Years do odd things to identity.
What does it mean to say
I am that child in the photograph
at Kishamish in 1935?
Might as well say I am the shadow
of a leaf of the acacia tree
felled seventy years ago
moving on the page the child reads.
Might as well say I am the words she read
or the words I wrote in other years,
flicker of shade and sunlight
as the wind moves through the leaves.

The Last Visit

In the heart of my memory, that house,
memories overcame me.
Only if I could forget them
would I be there, in that house.

There where all I remembered
was substance visible,
I was my shadow's shadow,
a child, a visitor, a ghost.

Where the ways grew narrow

Where the ways grew narrow
there above the sea,
tall flowers of yarrow
brushed against my knee.

All I have kept
from a time of sorrow:
a cold twilight
and the white yarrow.

The Desert Crossing

A wrinkled, spotted, pallid hide
stretched and sagging on a shack of bones
was her house now, her shaky tent
set up each day a little farther on
into the plain of thorns and dunes.
An awkward load to carry, so the way
was always farther between the springs of water.
The great silence lay behind each dune
like a lion with a woman's head. She sang
in a voice like wind in sand, a long
answer to the question that it did not ask.

Walking the Maze

The bright, broad earth dims to become
a labyrinth in which I walk
on feet that ache, grow numb,
and yet must feel the way I take.
Stumbling me on where I can't see,
step by step they make the road
I'm not quite sure is there. Unsure, unshod,
and slow, afraid to fall, I go
where all is now opaque
to me. Does the way lead out or in?
At the center, or the door, will I be free?
No choices left to make. I follow on
the maze whose gate and goal are mystery.

Desire and Fear

A willingness to die is my desire,
        not of the mind alone
but of the weary heart and weakened bone.
My fear is that the body, always wanting more,
        will clutch at flames of fire
sooner than leave me free to go
        on through the open door.

The Combat

On the farthest margin of old age
in thickets and quicksands of half-sleep
the fat grey serpent of despair
wrestles with the thin tiger of my rage.

The tiger's teeth meet in the snake.
Break, writhing backbone, break!

"Soul clap hands and louder sing" said Yeats

but the song this old soul wants to sing is soft,
like a child playing alone in a sunlit loft
with a long story she wants to tell,
singing it softly all to herself,
long, long, soft, soft.

Ancestry

I am such a long way from my ancestors now
in my extreme old age that I feel more one of them
than their descendant. Time comes round
in a bodily way I do not understand. Age undoes itself
and plays the Ouroboros. I the only daughter
have always been one of the tiny grandmothers,
laughing at everything, uncomprehending,
incomprehensible.

On the Western Shore

Ebb tide is when to roam
the long beach alone
and find the jetsam
of the forgotten or unknown,
a slender breastbone,
a glass net-float lost
from a boat off Honshu
borne over ocean
a century unbroken.

The lowest, the neap tide,
that bares long reaches
that were deep underwater
where the slope grows steep,
is when to walk out so far
that looking back you see
no shore. Under bare feet
the sand is bare and rippled. Dark
of evening deepens into night
and the sea becomes sleep.

～

Ursula Kroeber Le Guin (1929–2018) was a celebrated and beloved author of twenty-one novels, eleven volumes of short stories, four collections of essays, twelve children's books, six volumes of poetry, and four books of translation. The breadth and imagination of her work earned her five Nebulas and five Hugos, along with the PEN/Malamud and many other awards. In 2014 she was awarded the National Book Foundation Medal for Distinguished Contribution to American Letters, and in 2016 joined the short list of authors to be published in their lifetimes by the Library of America.

The book you are holding is a testament to the diverse community of passionate readers who supported "Ursula K. Le Guin: A Poet's Legacy." Copper Canyon Press is deeply grateful to the following individuals around the world whose philanthropic vision and love of poetry made this legacy collection possible. We have published *So Far So Good* together. Thank you!

Anonymous (3)
Teresa Aguiar
Gwyn Allman
Rick Alonso
Zaina Alrujaib
Hana Al-Sharif
Elissa Altman
Sarah Amberg
Sharon Amdall
Janet Eulalia Anderson
Richard Andrews
Annalee & Britt
Donald G.
 Armbruster Jr.
Janeen Armstrong
Karin Lisa Atkinson
Colt "Revlis Risling"
 Baker
Gregory Barbee
Ariana Barkley
Fayaway & Hermester
 Barrington
Hathaway Barry
Ellen Bass
Peter Bauman
Thomas Bayard
Catherine Ursula
 Becker
Donna & Matt Bellew
Lara Beneshan

Jake Bennet
Kitty Bergel
Erik & Erica Bergmann
Dana Bettinger
Mark Bibbins
Sarah Bird
Marlene Blessing
In memory of
 Mary Edge Blewett
Tara Bloyd
Twanna P. Bolling
Marianne Boruch
Ken Bowden
Katrina Gerhard
 Boyajian
Charles Boyce
Richard A. Brait
John William Branch
Electra Bratt
David Brewster
Enrico Brocardo
Joe & Maureen
 Brotherton
Jacob Bruner
Alex Buccieri
Deborah Buchanan
Vincent T. Buck
Jane & Vincent Buck
Angie Bucknell
bill burns

Bobette Buster
Catherine Butler
Patrick Byrnes
Mike Cadden
Valerie B. Caldwell
June Annette Cann
Steven Caplow
Alan S. Carroll
Tim & Sarah Cavanaugh
Barbara Center
In memory of
 Roxanne Chen
Justin Chimka
Eileen Chow
Lawrence Chung
Nathan Clum
Bonnie Gaia Colby
Michele Combs
Dom Conlon
Daphne Cooluris &
 Michael Doherty
Janet Cox
In honor of
 Janet Trask Cox
Tonaya Craft
In memory of
 Argentina Daley
Adriana Damiani
Susan DeWitt Davie
Page Dawsey

THANK YOU

Rowan Dent
Joseph J. De Salvo
Dennis de Vries
Jennifer Detres
Janice & Ray Dickeman
Min Min Dippold
Sarah Dodder
Don't You Feel It Too?
Jack Duffy &
 Eileen Kiera
Duygu & Dwayne
Vasiliki Dwyer
Catherine Edwards
Emily Ellerbe
Carol Ellis
Elaina Ellis
Tóth Endre
Kelsey Englert
Thomas Enochs
C. Jane Epperson
Laurie & Oskar Eustis
Michael Everson
 (Tregayata)
Nancy M. Faaren
Jeffrey Farrington
Liz Feder
Michael Ferris
Peter ffoulkes
Jay Fier
Selene Fisher
Mel Flannery
With love for Kelly
 Forsythe
Bob & Kathy Francis
John Freeman
Loretta Gase
Mimi Gardner Gates
Robert "Bob" Geballe
Zahreen Ghaznavi
Chand Svare Ghei
Nancy Gifford

London W. Gillean
Wren Godwin
David Goodman
Great Men/Great MDs:
 TKA & DA
Caroline Grebbell
Deborah S. Green
Kip Greenthal
Bill Griffin
Emily Grise
Martha A. Habecker
Richard Alan Hadfield
Art Hanlon
John Harmon
C.R. Harper
Cyd Harrell
Phyllis Hatfield
Anne C. Heller
Jennifer Jeane
 Hildebrandt
Stephen D. Hill
Emily Hoechst
Brett Hornby
Auke Hulst
C. Hume
Russel Hunter, DVM
Milla Ikonen
Rob Jacques
Jade
Sol Johnson
Thomas M. Johnson
Lena Jonsson
Kristen Jorgensen
Adam E. Justice-Mills
K.D.
Eric L. Kellerman
Patrick Gage Kelley
PJ Kendrick
Cheryl Dianne Carter
 Kern
KG of Ethos Books

Lisa & Bart Klingler
Tricia Knoll
Taroh Kogure
Cory & Katie Kohn
Barbara H. Kovaz
Kenneth Kreer
Carolyn
 Kreiter-Foronda
Akira Kuroda
Afshan Lakha
Deborah Landau
Justine Lattimer
A. Lee
Hongwoo Lee
Maureen Lee &
 Mark Busto
Cat Leja
James P. Lenfestey
Carol & Geo Levin
Robin Levin
Winnie Lim
Jayne Lindley
Mary Jeanne Linford
Michael Little
In Memory of Susan
 Lockwood
Thomas &
 Julie Lombardo
Branon Lyle
Sallie Rose Madrone
Susan C. Maresco
Alexis & Dolores Marks
In honor of Wayne &
 Doris Martin
Allison Mascolo
Elizabeth Jeanne
 Mattson
Teresa Mayberg
James McAninch
Brendan Taylor
 McClure
James McCorkle

THANK YOU

Robert & Bobbi McCoy

Lylianna Allala &
Josh McCran

JoAnne McFarland

Stephanie McMahon

In memory of Timothy
Carey McShane

Richard Merrifield

Laura & David Midgley

Michael Miller

Gerard Yee Hock Min

Matthew Sonshine
Moore

Susan Leslie Moore

Joan Moritz

Diana Morley

Elizabeth Douglas
Mornin

Kate Morris

Barbara Morrison

Lisa Morrow

Michael Mueller-Hayes

Leslie J. Muir

Isabel de Navasqüés y
de Urquijo

Andronikos Nedos

Kay H. Neill

Kayla Marrie Odell

John Phillips & Anne
O'Donnell

Yu Okubo

Patrick O'Leary

Betty Rae Olson

Christopher E.
O'Malley

Anh Que On

Sharon L. Oriel

Michael & Joylee Ort

Connie Ozer

H. C. Palmer

LynnMarie Panzarino

Catherine Patrick

Robert B. Patton

Tonia L. Payne

Anne Payne Barker

Anastasia Pease

Peter Pereira

George Peter "Dad"

Justin Peters

Snow Brook Peterson

Kurt Phillips

John Pierce

Kimberly
Pittman-Schulz

Jörg "Patterner" Plate

Joe & Pansy Polatti

Edward G. Popham

Katherine Prevost

Alana Yu-lan Price

John Price

Sterling Price

For Quinn & Ainsley

Geila Rajaee

Barbra & Adrian Ramos

Steve Rawls

Emily & Dan Raymond

Michele RC

Alvaro Rebon

Hula, Eva Genevieve &
Stella Marlene Reece

Ohana Resnick

Katt & Scott Rewerts

Logan Valerie Ringle

Robert Riordan

Sara & Tripp Ritter

Kim Jamison Rivera

Tom Robbins

Rebecca Robinson

Byron Robitaille

Rocky Mountain Land
Library

Jude Rosenberg

Mioto Rouch

The Rubinfeld Family

Jill Ruckelshaus &
Bill Ruckelshaus Jr.

Pamela Sampel

Paul Sarvasy &
Sheila Sondik

Cherie R. Savy

Eulalie & Carlo
Scandiuzzi

Facundo Martín
Scavuzzo

Susan Schaefer
Bernardo

In honor of Inge
Schneider

Margaret Schonfield

Seagull Books

Kim & Jeff Seely

Dr. Nina Semjonous

Silky Shah

Mike Shema

Peter M. Sidell

Rick Simonson

Norman Sinel

Claudia Skelton

Joseph A. Slotnick

Jeremy Adam Smith

Kevin Smith

Randall Steven Smith

Rosemary Hirst Smith

Sandra M. Sohr

Rob Spampinato

Per Stalby

Diana Steele

Melissa Stein

Jim Straus

Steve Straus

Susan Straus

Meralee Street

Victor Stringer

Tsitika H. Sussman

George & Kim Suyama

THANK YOU

Jennifer K. Swank
James Swinterton
Arthur Sze
Trias
William & Ruth True
S. Ali Tucker
  Lichtenstein
Chase Twichell
Maria Van Newkirk
Jessica Vandervoort
Cato Vandrare
Lisa & Sam Verhovek
John Waclawski
Dan Waggoner

Wee Heavy
  Walter-Stern
Stephe Watson & Sarah
  Love Schwartz
Robert Weissburg
Chris Welch
Jon S. Wenrick
Bill Whiteman
Jan & Bob Whitsitt
Ella Wiegers
Michael Wiegers
In memory of Alie
  Wiegersma Smaalders
J. L. Wieringa

D. D. Wigley
For Wil
Lance Wilcox
Samuel A. Wilkinson III
rhonda anne winter
Paul Woodruff
Beffa Ommaya
  Wyldemoon
Maccewill J.D. Yip
Dean Young
Emma Ziker

Poetry is vital to language and living. Since 1972, Copper Canyon Press has published extraordinary poetry from around the world to engage the imaginations and intellects of readers, writers, booksellers, librarians, teachers, students, and donors.

WE ARE GRATEFUL FOR THE MAJOR SUPPORT PROVIDED BY:

THE PAUL G. ALLEN
FAMILY FOUNDATION

TO LEARN MORE ABOUT UNDERWRITING
COPPER CANYON PRESS TITLES,
PLEASE CALL 360-385-4925 EXT. 103

WE ARE GRATEFUL FOR THE MAJOR SUPPORT PROVIDED BY:

Anonymous

Jill Baker and Jeffrey Bishop

Anne and Geoff Barker

Donna and Matt Bellew

John Branch

Diana Broze

Sarah and Tim Cavanaugh

Beatrice R. and Joseph A. Coleman
    Foundation

Laurie and Oskar Eustis

Mimi Gardner Gates

Linda Gerrard and Walter Parsons

Nancy Gifford

Gull Industries Inc. on behalf of
    Ruth and William True

The Trust of Warren A. Gummow

Phil Kovacevich and Eric Wechsler

Lakeside Industries Inc. on behalf
    of Jeanne Marie Lee

Maureen Lee and Mark Busto

Rhoady Lee and Alan Gartenhaus

Ellie Mathews and Carl Youngmann
    as The North Press

Anne O'Donnell and John Phillips

Petunia Charitable Fund and
    adviser Elizabeth Hebert

Gay Phinney

Suzie Rapp and Mark Hamilton

Emily and Dan Raymond

Jill and Bill Ruckelshaus

Kim and Jeff Seely

Richard Swank

University Research Council of
    DePaul University

Vincentian Endowment Foundation

Dan Waggoner

Caleb Young and Keep It Cinematic

The dedicated interns and
    faithful volunteers of
    Copper Canyon Press